BRITISH RAILWAYS

SOUTHERN REGION

in Colour

For the Modeller and Historian

KEVIN ROBERTSON

Ian Allan

PUBLISHING

CONTENTS

Title page:
A wonderful panoramic view of Brighton shed on 12 April 1958 with both steam and diesel power present. Standing out amongst a veritable sea of black is the restored Adams 'T3' class 4-4-0 No 563, together with the 'Terrier' 0-6-0 tank repainted in LBSCR colours for use as the Brighton Works shunter. Most of the tank engines visible would also appear to be of former LBSCR vintage, although it is possible to recognise a solitary LSWR 'M7'. *Tony Molyneaux*

Above:
A rare visitor to Eastleigh depot was this 'C2X' class 0-6-0, No 32437, possibly having just received attention in the nearby works. For most of its time during BR days, this engine was based at Brighton, although its final year was spent at Feltham. *Bob Winkworth collection*

First published 2007

ISBN (10) 0 7110 3233 5
ISBN (13) 978 0 7110 3233 0

Published by Ian Allan Publishing Ltd, Hersham, Surrey, KT12 4RG

Printed in England by Ian Allan Publishing Ltd, Hersham, Surrey, KT12 4RG

Code: 0711/C1

Visit the Ian Allan Publishing website at www.ianallanpublishing.com

INTRODUCTION

So what is it about the Southern that appeals to the enthusiast? Many refer to the plethora of Pacifics which were active on the Bournemouth line until the summer of 1967. Others perhaps, take a different view, preferring instead the rustic charm of the numerous branch lines that spread out from, or fed into (depending upon one's viewpoint) the main routes. A further group may hold sway to the third-rail electric services. The Southern Railway was a pioneer of these in the carriage of the masses, although many years later such services would also become an embarrassment. Whatever the personal preference it can be truly said the Southern had it all.

Looking back then over the decades it is also tempting to revere the past through rose-tinted spectacles. Indeed, the past was supposedly when the sun always shone and the trains ran on time. However, a little study will reveal such a perspective was perhaps not quite the case, as consistently within the weekly special traffic notices of the 1950s were comments from headquarters as to poor timekeeping and punctuality. Just 50-60% appears to have been the average for on-time running so far as steam services were concerned. All this of course, gave ammunition to those who would later discredit steam as both unreliable and outmoded.

But these words are not intended to be a political discourse or a personal perspective upon the rights and wrongs of the railway network of years ago. Instead, and as referred to in the title, its purpose is to present what I sincerely trust will be seen as an attractive series of colour illustrations, most hopefully new to the reader, and which are intended to portray the Southern scene for the benefit of the enthusiast. Whether that enthusiasm manifests itself in model form or simply within the armchair, it matters not, just as long as it is enjoyed.

As an independent company, the Southern Railway was better at some things than its neighbouring privately owned railways pre-1948, and to be fair, worse at other matters. Nationalisation was intended to take the best of each and weld these into a cohesive and efficient network. Sadly, that could never happen as long as equipment dating back to pre-Nationalisation days was in use, and it would not be until the standardisation of modern motive power throughout the network from the mid to late 1960s onwards, that any real benefit began to be felt.

Even then the Southern was independent, pursuing a policy of third-rail electrification when others were opting for the arguably more efficient, although initially more expensive, ac overhead electric transmission. Likewise, it would take decades of public ownership to remove the vestiges of the former administration and which to be fair, were sometimes destroyed in almost wanton vandalism rather than any attempt to adapt older structures for a newer use.

Simultaneous with the end of steam often came the closure of various branch lines over which such steam services had also operated, while changing traffic needs also saw the demise of what had once been regular workings. Accordingly, the annual hop-pickers specials of Kent had disappeared by the 1960s, while at the opposite end of the Southern system, the lines west of Exeter were slowly being culled by their new owner, the Western Region.

All this would also have a bearing on what was recorded by the photographers of the period. For a start, colour film was expensive and transport for the photographer was invariably by train itself; the days of private motoring for all were still a few years away. Then there were the type of subjects to be covered. Some topics have always been more popular and hence a Bulleid Pacific dashing along at speed was far more likely to be recorded than a humble goods engine shunting at a wayside station.

Some routes too were more popular than others. Lines on which steam was generally in use drew more photographers than those on which the then new green electrics were running. It is ironic of course, that years on it is with just as much enthusiasm that views of the 'green era' electrics are sought. All this is mentioned for a reason – I am quite sure the reader will have gathered that as well!

In a title such as that chosen by the publisher for the present work, it would first be impossible to cover every aspect, location and type of stock operating on the Southern in what is a limited number of pages. Additionally, there is a finite number of unpublished colour slides, and I have made a conscious decision not to attempt to replicate what I know has been seen before.

Even so, I have been very fortunate to have access to much new and unpublished material, although, and I make no excuses, there must be gaps in coverage where the general subject area is so vast.

As in the companion volume also on the Western Region by Laurence Waters, I have ensured the content does not cease either at the end of steam. Thus, where the general Southern scene remained unaltered after that fateful day in July 1967 when steam working on the Southern Region ceased, a number of views are included to depict the railway over several decades. I am sure many reading this will indeed recall, as I do, scenes such as those seen here.

Aside also from the locomotives and trains, which do of course make up the majority of this work, I have included a number of infrastructure views, which I hope depict the scene as it was, before the changes that have resulted in today's railway.

Today the Southern is no longer a railway of Bulleid designs, 4-COR units, and pneumatic signals operating between Basingstoke and Brookwood. Instead, we have a modern railway network carrying thousands daily on a route system laid down in the 19th century. Modern units convey passengers in air-conditioned comfort past colour light signals operating on bi-directional signalled lines, much beyond the comprehension of the steam era, but perhaps not totally beyond the vision of the likes of Sir Herbert Walker, or Oliver Bulleid.

The Southern then has come of age. Its legacy must be what is now simply an extensive suburban and outer suburban network. Technology may have compressed the time taken to travel, but in so doing it has also lost its individuality. It is this individuality that the following pages seek to recapture. The days of green and steam, the days when the Southern could perhaps be said to be as independent and individualistic as its neighbour at Paddington.

Kevin Robertson
September 2007

Right:
Think of the Southern Region in the lifetime of most steam enthusiasts, and the prospect of a Bulleid Pacific probably comes to mind – rebuilt or original – according to choice. It is difficult to add something new to the thousands of words already expounded on these machines, and so perhaps the best thing is to simply let the pictures do the talking! One of these fine locomotives, Rebuilt 'Battle of Britain' No 34088 *213 Squadron,* seems to be almost straining at the leash as it awaits departure from Basingstoke with a down West of England line service.

The front end corner of a green-liveried WR DMU on the Basingstoke–Reading service can just be seen in the distance, left. On the extreme left are the remains of the old GWR station – hence the lower quadrant ringed-arm signal. The canopies too display considerable differences; that on the left of the main station dates from the original stopping place, while on the right is the 20th century rebuild. Such was the Southern scene in the early to mid-1960s, soon to be swept away with the extension of third-rail electrification to Bournemouth.
Collection Tony Woodford

Below:
Also at Basingstoke, and unfortunately on an unrecorded date, was this unusual sight of three Rebuilt Bulleid Pacifics all heading in the same direction. Only the nearest can be positively identified as *602 Squadron* which was No 34089. The second is a 'West Country' the third is another 'Battle of Britain'. The gantry of semaphores would be replaced in 1966 with the commissioning of the new panel box, which was in turn due to be superseded in 2007.
Tony Woodford collection

Above:
Rebuilt 'Merchant Navy' No 35004 *Cunard White Star* is seen near Totton with an up Bournemouth line express complete with red and cream BR Mk1 stock. This engine was widely regarded as one of the best of the class then remaining in service. Unfortunately, its career came to a sudden end when it broke the tyre off the front left-side driving wheel, due to a violent bout of slipping near Hook. As a result it was towed to Eastleigh and condemned on the spot. At this time, repairs were no longer being authorised and in this damaged condition it was not deemed suitable to be taken any further and was cut up in front of the running shed early in 1966. *Paul Bodkin*

Below:
Pushed perhaps slightly from the limelight by the veritable army of Pacifics the 'Schools' class 4-4-0s nevertheless performed feats often equal to the larger machines until rendered redundant in 1962. For the last few years of their life several were based at Nine Elms from where they regularly worked Basingstoke and Lymington services, as well as on occasions, as far west as Salisbury. Seen here is No 30911 *Dover* in company with 'E4' class 0-6-2T No 32498 in September 1959. At this time, No 30911 was on paper at least, still allocated to Ramsgate but was surplus to requirements there due to the recent electrification of the Kent Coast lines. *Bob Winkworth collection*

Above:

For working the Hayling Island branch, where a weight restriction over the timber bridge at Langstone precluded anything larger, a number of the diminutive 'A1X' class 0-6-0Ts were retained at Fratton shed on the outskirts of Southsea. In their final years the 'Terriers' had the distinction of being the oldest steam engines at work on British Railways, some dating back to the 1870s. This particular example, No 32650, had been built at Brighton in 1876 and had previously seen service on the Isle of Wight as No W9 *Fishbourne*. Numbered by BR as shown it was withdrawn when the Hayling Island route was closed, in November 1963. It is now preserved on the Spa Valley Railway at Tunbridge Wells. *Tony Woodford collection*

Left:

This in the days before the Swanage branch became a heritage railway with the unmistakable architecture of what was then the one intermediate stopping place at Corfe Castle, recorded on 15 March 1963. Still in place were the typical green signs, while the mediæval castle after which the village and station are named can just be glimpsed in the background behind the trees. The view is looking north, up, towards Worgret Junction and the main line. *John Bailey*

Right:

To the uninitiated, the idea of a Southern route running through anything other than fields and pasture land may appear strange, with the idea of industry and clutter seemingly confined to lines in the Midlands and North. Here, on the outskirts of Southampton, we disprove the concept, the train hauled by 'Merchant Navy' No 35029 *Ellerman Lines* slowly negotiating the sharp curve from Northam Junction and heading west towards Southampton Tunnel and Central station on 6 November 1960. The signals are the up home from Tunnel Junction, that to the left taking services north towards Eastleigh while to the right is the curve to Southampton Terminus. Beneath are co-acting arms and a banner repeater for the service operated by No 35029 is located on the reverse side of the lower bracket. *John Bailey*

Below:

The architectural style of the railways has changed considerably over the years. This attractive example is the exterior of Woolston station on the Southampton–Fareham line via Netley. A more modern building style, perhaps not so pleasing on the eye, and unconnected with the railway, is visible in the shape of the tower block left, fronting International Way on the Weston estate, as seen on 22 December 1963. *John Bailey*

Above:
The transition from steam: green-liveried BRCW Type 3 'Crompton' (later Class 33) No D6523 heads a through train to Lymington from Waterloo and is just passing Lymington Junction signalbox on 27 July 1963. This was the point of divergence for the single-track branch just west of Brockenhurst, and until 1966, was the point where the Ringwood route branched off through Holmsley. Consequent upon the withdrawal of the 'Schools' class the previous year, 1963 was the first time diesels had had charge of the through trains, with the advantage that a change of engine was now no longer required at Brockenhurst. *John Bailey*

Left:
The closure of many lines in the 1960s often coincided with the demise of the steam engine. This is East Grinstead High Level with the diverging lines to Three Bridges and St Margaret's Junction. Services here ceased from 2 January 1967. *Tony Goodyear*

ON THE MAIN LINE

Right:
Having already glimpsed part of the areas it is intended to cover within this volume, we now look again at the main line services. One of the best-known trains on the Southern was for many years the 'Golden Arrow', which is seen here at Shakespeare Tunnel near Folkestone, behind No 34088 *213 Squadron* on 21 July 1960. The coal train passing alongside could well be from one of the Kent collieries, several of which were still active at this time. Stewarts Lane depot provided the engine for the 'Arrow', which survived beyond the end of steam although in its final years the Pullman complement had been reduced to just a few vehicles.
Tony Molyneaux

Below:
Over 100 miles west of the previous view another Rebuilt Bulleid Pacific, this time No 34082 *615 Squadron*, is seen working a down West of England service through Tisbury on 29 August 1964. Not long after, diesels began to encroach on these services, commensurate with the transfer of the former LSWR route between Salisbury and Exeter to Western Region control. On the extreme right is the end of the former LSWR van that was a static feature of the station for many years. It is illustrated later. *Tony Molyneaux*

Above:
Maroon coaches were seen on Southern lines on the various through workings from the London Midland and Eastern Regions, the most prodigious service of which was undoubtedly the 'Pines Express', seen here heading north at Basingstoke and far from its original route via the Somerset & Dorset and Bath. (The 'Pines' had been re-routed away from the S&D after the end of the 1962 summer timetable which was destined to be a precursor to the eventual run down and closure of the S&D line.) In charge is a filthy 'Battle of Britain' class rebuilt Pacific, the blue background to the nameplate identifying the engine type, but not the locomotive itself. *Tony Woodford collection*

Below:
A delightful view of 'Merchant Navy' No 35024 *East Asiatic Company* climbing the 1-in-106 bank towards Battledown Flyover near Basingstoke, with a Waterloo service. Although undated, the inclusion of the mixed, early BR-liveried coaches allied to the green probably dates this to not long after the engine had been rebuilt at Eastleigh Works in April 1959. *Tony Woodford collection*

Right:
It would be wrong to imply that in BR days all Southern main line passenger trains were in the hands of Bulleid Pacifics as for many years, the various Maunsell types could be seen on perhaps not the top link duties, but certainly semi-fast and stopping services. One of the Eastleigh 'King Arthur' class 4-6-0s is seen here at Basingstoke as No 30448 *Sir Tristram* waits to depart with a Salisbury service. The number 852 on the end of the coach indicates this rake is a three-coach Bulleid set dating from 1951. *Tony Woodford collection*

Below:
By 1962, withdrawal of most of the 'Lord Nelson' class 4-6-0s meant the Pacifics were now in sole charge of the numerous boat trains between Waterloo and Southampton. No 34031 *Torrington* was recorded on the up fast line just north of Allbrook (Eastleigh) with a service emanating from the vessel SS *United States* on 23 May 1962. Typical of these services were the parcels vans necessary for the copious luggage involved. The up boat trains were also a source of difficulties for the railway control office as the scheduling had to be flexible according to the time taken for the liner to arrive, allied to associated unloading and customs clearance. For this reason there were a number of spare 'Q' paths available which were intended to be used for these services without causing interruption to the normal scheduled trains. *Tony Molyneaux*

Left:
Casting a plume of smoke obliterating the up line signal gantry, another Rebuilt 'West Country' class engine, this time No 34034 *Honiton*, leaves Farnborough with a semi-fast from the Salisbury line on 9 May 1961. At this time the signals on this stretch of railway were a mixture of mechanical and semi-automatic low-pressure pneumatic semaphores, the latter dating from LSWR days which remained in use until ousted by MAS in 1965/6. *Paul Bodkin*

Below:
The classic view of Bournemouth Central from the east end of the station with No 34089 *602 Squadron* seemingly with steam to spare as it sets off on the 100-mile journey to Waterloo. The two centre lines were through routes having no platform faces, but were also used for stock storage and light engine movements. With electrification and the end of steam these lines were considered redundant and were lifted, although the empty space that was left has never been easy to use and decades later remains as a gaunt reminder of busier times. *Bob Winkworth collection*

Above:
The evening sun catches the side of
'Lord Nelson' No 30862 *Lord Collingwood*
as it pounds up the 1-in-250 gradient
north of Winchester with an evening
boat train on 19 June 1961. Eastleigh
was responsible for the motive power
for most of these workings. *John Bailey*

Right:
The down gantry at Southampton Central
as seen from the west end of Platform 4
on 14 June 1959. The train standing at
Platform 3 is the 11.15am Portsmouth to
Cardiff service which will travel via Salisbury
and Westbury. In charge is BR Standard
Class 5 4-6-0 No 73112. Platforms 2 and 3,
which fronted the centre island platform,
were usually reserved for the semi-fast
and cross-country services in either direction.
John Bailey

Above:
Sadly, the 1950 art-deco Southampton Ocean Terminal is nowadays but a memory, its life curtailed consequent upon the rapid displacement of ocean liner travel by the jet airliner which occurred within just two decades of the terminal building being opened. Despite much local protest the structure was razed to the ground in 1983, so while the occasional boat train still enters the docks today, they can no longer pull up alongside the building as seen here. This is No 34071 *601 Squadron* awaiting its next move, recorded on 8 April 1961.
Tony Molyneaux

Below:
A Rebuilt 'Merchant Navy' in full flight south of Shawford on the four-track section between that station and Eastleigh. In the background is Bowker's footbridge, which was unfortunately a private access way otherwise it would have made for a wonderful vantage point for photographers. *Tony Molyneaux*

Above:
The unmistakable location of Southampton Central, with No 34098 *Templecombe* having passed the home signals at 'on' but no doubt under the direction of the hand-signalman on the ground, on 5 September 1964. The train is destined for Bournemouth and has the duty number hung on the front of the smokebox. To the right the pair of rusty sidings were once used for coal traffic destined for the nearby power station. *Tony Molyneaux*

Below:
In the days when pre-Grouping and pre-Nationalisation locomotive types were still charged with semi-fast workings, 4-6-0 No 30745 *Tintagel* waits at Woking on a mixed rake of stock sometime in 1955. This was one of the batch of Robert Urie-designed 'King Arthur' class engines, withdrawals of which were already taking place at this time. No 30745 was removed from stock in February 1956. *Bob Winkworth collection*

Above:
Much of the steam-era railway disappeared almost at the same time as the engines themselves, one example being the camping coaches which were to be found placed on stub sidings at popular tourist destinations. Included in these was Beaulieu Road in the New Forest, where the main subject is 'Merchant Navy' No 35030, formerly carrying the name *Elder Dempster Lines*, and about to leave westwards with what, from the headcode at least, is an inter-regional service. In the up platform, left is the tail end of a new, blue-liveried 'TC', trailer corridor set.
Dave Waldron

Left:
Pounding through the New Forest near Brockenhurst, No 34017 *Ilfracombe* has charge of a Waterloo–Bournemouth working on 2 July 1966. During the summer months much of the forest area was often tinder-box dry, and with the propensity of the Bulleid breed towards the throwing of sparks and cinders, Waterloo was regularly involved with claims for fire damage compensation, even if they knew these were not always genuine.
Tony Molyneaux

Above:
Slightly unusual motive power, in the form of ex-LMS 'Black 5' No 44942 recorded between Swaythling and Southampton Airport with a Bournemouth–York working on 30 April 1966. It is possible the engine had earlier worked through to the Southern with the corresponding down working, although it was also not unknown for Bournemouth (or any of the other steam sheds) to 'borrow' an engine to cover what would otherwise be a gap in their availability.
Tony Molyneaux

Above:
A beautifully clean No 34064 *Fighter Command* on what was reported as a down boat train for the *Iberia*, near Shawford on 9 June 1962. Once upon a time the headboards for a number of the boat trains were stored in a grounded carriage body outside the front of Eastleigh shed, probably a dozen or more, but few appear to have survived.
Tony Molyneaux

Left:
With the gradient post indicative of a falling grade, No 34093 *Saunton* speeds down the bank north of Winchester with the 8.27am Waterloo departure for Weymouth on 9 September 1961. Until the 1930s there had been an intermediate signalbox here called Worthy, located close by the site of the permanent way hut.
Tony Molyneaux

Below:
Another boat train, but this time emanating from Weymouth. No 34060 *25 squadron* is seen north of Allbrook (Eastleigh) with the service on 15 June 1964. Originally, Channel Islands boat trains from Weymouth had run via Castle Cary, Westbury and along the WR main line to Paddington, but a change of regional boundaries saw these transferred to Southern operation some years earlier. The mile posts at Weymouth still show the route length from Paddington (168m 63c) rather than from Waterloo (142m 64c) despite being replaced by modern-style signs in recent years. *Tony Molyneaux*

Above:
A much cleaner Rebuilt 'West Country', No 34017 *Ilfracombe* passes through Micheldever at speed on 2 July 1961, bound for Bournemouth. Here at Micheldever, there were a number of sidings used for the storage of carriage stock awaiting works attention although unfortunately, the first attention they usually received was from the vandals. Much chalk had been hewn from the area in the early part of the 20th century which was used as infill for expansion at Southampton Docks. For many years also, the cutting at Micheldever had been the site of a large oil storage and distribution terminal which lasted beyond the steam era, but has now been out of use for some years. *Tony Molyneaux*

Right:
In original form before rebuilding, No 34005 *Barnstaple* was recorded at Swaythling heading south, probably around 1956. The houses in the background lasted until the 1980s when road improvements in the area resulted in them being displaced in favour of a dual-carriageway. There is an ATC battery box on the front framing; not all Bulleid types were so fitted. *John Bailey*

Above:

A rarer sight was BR Standard '9F' class 2-10-0 No 92205, entering Southampton Central at the head of what was recorded by the photographer as a 21-bogie van train forming a pigeon special. This was on 2 June 1963 and no doubt the photographer had been given prior notice of the working. Pigeon specials were more common on the Southern off the former Somerset & Dorset line and would usually only venture as far as Christchurch, being berthed in the yard and remains of the former route to Ringwood. In addition, smaller volumes of the birds were regularly received at a number of stations and released by the local porter, according to the instructions on the label attached to the bird basket. *John Bailey*

Below:

A cold winter's day finds an intrepid photographer recording the progress of No 34031 *Torrington* as it speeds through Shawford for Southampton, possibly in the winter of 1963. The main lines here are to the left, with the track to the right being a loop running from Shawford Junction, at this time only accessible for down trains from Winchester Chesil station. *John Bailey*

Right:
Warmer times, and No 34041 *Wilton* cautiously exits the New, or Western Docks at Southampton on to the up main line with a boat train, this one from the *Oriana* on 28 July 1961. *Tony Molyneaux*

Below:
The final outing: No 34021, formerly named *Dartmoor*, runs light through Basingstoke on Sunday, 9 July 1967 carrying a West of England headcode. The engine was destined for Salisbury where it was withdrawn upon arrival, steam being abolished on Southern metals from midnight. *Dave Waldron*

Left:

The prestige train on the Southern's Western section in later years was the 'Bournemouth Belle', usually given to haulage by a 'Merchant Navy' class engine, but seen here in the hands of Rebuilt 'Battle of Britain' No 34077 *603 Squadron* near Allbrook on 30 May 1964. The provision of the WR-liveried parcels van came about as a replacement for the former Pullman brake second vehicles which were due to be withdrawn. Their replacements were due to former Pullman employee Charles Long, who while standing on Clapham Junction station one day, saw a vehicle of this type in chocolate and cream livery passing through from the Western Region. It was then but a small step for the Southern Region to acquire two such vehicles which remained with the 'Belle' set until the service was withdrawn. *Tony Molyneaux*

Below:

This boat train is complete with a 'Union Castle' headboard, even though it is as late as 27 April 1967. No 34044 *Woolacombe* is slowly entering the old, Eastern Docks from alongside Southampton Terminus with a mixed rake including a new-liveried blue and grey coach. This rolling stock livery hardly seemed to fit in with the steam railway. Alongside is one of the diesel shunters then being used in the docks, although their tenure would be brief as a result of the mass containerisation taking place. *Tony Molyneaux*

Left:
A mixed rake behind No 34089 *602 Squadron* is seen on 18 June 1967 during the last RCTS excursion over the southern using steam. The location is the heathland of the Swanage branch near to Corfe Castle and the footplate is host to at least two unofficial visitors. On the rear of the train it is just possible to glimpse a BR Class 4 tank engine No 80146, ready to haul the train back from Swanage as there was never a facility to turn an engine of the size of a 'West Country' Pacific at the terminus. *Tony Molyneaux*

Left:
This service was reported as a Royal Mail Line boat train and is depicted south of Shawford with No 34088 *213 Squadron* in charge on 12 September 1965. The first vehicle is of Bulleid stock and still has its original set number, '844', visible on the end which indicates it was part of a three-coach rake. *Tony Molyneaux*

Left:
BR Standard Class 5 4-6-0 No 73155 nears Lymington Junction west of Brockenhurst with a down Bournemouth service. Some crews preferred the Class 5s for their predictable performance although by this time, 1966, they were also becoming run down which accentuated the hard riding qualities of the class. The bottom of the smokebox door has been scorched.
Tony Molyneaux

INFRASTRUCTURE AND DETAILS

Left:
Having seen the various fast passenger workings, we now turn awhile to the stations where the trains called. The first of these is the seldom-photographed interior of Reading South. Here, the South Eastern met the Great Western although eventually the former SECR station would be closed and its traffic diverted to a pair of additional platform faces at Reading General (WR). The posters, telephone box, 'Brute' trolley and discarded sacks are all so typical of a scene that remained unchanging – or so it seemed, for many years. *Tony Woodford collection*

Below:
The unmistakable view of the down side at Winchester, complete with contemporary motor cars by Austin and Ford amongst others. The centre structure is of course the original building, with various add-ons either side. The clock was not original, but was provided some time in the 19th century, apparently after an incident involving a passenger and the Board of Trade. What actually occurred is now sadly lost in the mists of time. *Tony Woodford collection*

Above:
Continental ferry wagons are parked on the siding leading to the up side yard at Winchester. Beneath is the up side entrance and subway, altered considerably in the years since this view was taken. The station here is still open although the whole area formerly used as goods facilities has long since become a car park. *Doug Hannah*

Right:
A final view of Winchester, looking north towards Basingstoke from the vantage point of Upper High Street road bridge with the goods shed and yard on the left. The green covered structure on the right was a water tank feeding the columns at the end of each platform. Visible under the canopy, left, is the green-painted timber windbreak. This survived for many years and was unusual, but not unique to this station. *Tony Woodford collection*

Above:
The down side at Swaythling was the LSWR architecture style of 50 years later, in the 1880s. The platform was set some yards beyond the brick building and the timber platform shelter is visible on the right.
This design was to allow for an intended quadrupling of the tracks through here, which never came, but would have meant the brick structure was then correctly positioned for a re-sited down platform. *Paul Bodkin*

Below:
The grandiose exterior of Exmouth station with two Austin A40 cars prominent. (The author took his driving test in a car like this in 1969.) This was a rather imposing building for a seaside terminus and may well at one time have provided accommodation for the stationmaster as was common practice with the LSWR. There is an empty space on the top of the building where a clock no doubt once reposed.

At one time, Exmouth was the terminus for two lines arriving from different directions. From the north west was the route from Exeter through Topsham and diverging from the main line at the appropriately named Exmouth Junction. From the east came the branch from Sidmouth Junction via Ottery St Mary and Budleigh Salterton, from where another short line branched off to Sidmouth from Tipton St John's.
Tony Woodford collection

Above:

Similar in appearance to Winchester was the wayside station of Micheldever – originally called Andover Road. Here, the building is probably little altered from its construction, this being a view of the up-side structure. Later expansion here afforded both up and down loops as well as a new down platform, the through lines being without any platform faces. The loops no longer survive and instead, a new island platform was built in 1966/67 with the result that the building shown here, although still functioning as the main building and ticket office, no longer has an operational platform face.

Tony Woodford collection

Below:

A typical LSWR station scene was at Dunbridge between Romsey and Salisbury, viewed towards the west on 19 January 1963. The main structure clearly doubles as living accommodation while the signalbox beyond the level crossing is of typical LSWR design. For a short time under BR the station was renamed Mottisfont, a name once carried by a nearby stopping place on the long-closed branch to Andover.
A reversion has since been made to the original title.

John Bailey

Left:
This is another location where the building size appears to be outside all reasonable needs for the location, this being Netley on the coastal line between Southampton (St Denys) and Fareham. Traffic here was invariably local although it was of course not far from the renowned soft fruit area around Swanwick. Once upon a time there had also been a branch from Netley to the military hospital of the same name, which was still extant even if rarely used as late as the 1960s. *Paul Bodkin*

Below:
The distinctive architecture of Itchen Abbas station on the former Alton & Winchester Railway. Also known as the Mid-Hants line, part of the route still survives as today's preserved Mid-Hants Railway 'Watercress Line'. The station building served a dual role with accommodation for the stationmaster although by the time this view was taken on 1 May 1966, that particular grade had long been removed from the station.

Services through Itchen Abbas ceased in 1973 and the section from Alresford to Winchester Junction was abandoned completely. The station site has been cleared and the station building demolished to be replaced by a number of private houses. Similar station buildings survive at Alresford and Ropley on the MHR. Itchen Abbas station may be recalled as having one particular claim to fame as it was the starting place for the railway career of Sam Fay – later of course Sir Sam Fay – who went on to become the general manager of the Great Central Railway. *John Bailey*

INFRASTRUCTURE AND DETAILS

Above:
Moving west a few miles and this is the platform side of Stockbridge station, again deep in Hampshire, on 27 June 1964. The main building has been slate hung, probably as an additional means of weather protection, although this did little for the overall appearance. The canopy design is not original as this would have been hipped in its earliest days in the area of the exit from the booking hall. A similar style building survives at Haslemere. *John Bailey*

Above:
Further west still and this is Highbridge on the former Somerset & Dorset branch to Burnham-on-Sea. Many years earlier this had been the headquarters of the locomotive and carriage works of the S&DJR operated by the Southern and LMS, but was by now under the control of BR (LMR) and later (WR). *Tony Woodford collection*

Above and right:
The imposing structure of the former LSWR Goods Receiving Offices at the Barbican, Plymouth. Many years after the railway company had ceased to exist as an independent entity, and many decades also after the former SR had a presence in the city, its memory is perpetuated. It must be wondered how many people passing the building realise the significance of the wording? *Tony Woodford collection*

Right:
Back in Hampshire again we see Holmsley – known as Christchurch Road until February 1863, and located on the original Southampton & Dorchester Railway, known as the Castleman's Corkscrew. The view is primarily of the former up platform looking in the direction of Ringwood. In the foreground is the space where there had been sidings until 1961, although these, a loading dock, siding to the goods shed, and up sidings were out of use by this time. The view was taken on a damp Boxing Day in 1963 when the route had less than six months left to survive. Today, the main station building serves as a welcoming tearoom. *John Bailey*

Below:
The much-lamented terminus at Bournemouth West on another wet day complete with a collection of road vehicles including a number of Minis and at least one Austin. Here, trains would arrive from and depart for Bath while some London services also had a portion serving the station.

In addition, Bournemouth West was the terminus for local services to and from Southampton via Ringwood. Beyond the now long-demolished passenger station, were extensive carriage sidings. These have found a new use in recent times as stabling and servicing for the electric units operating on the main line. *Tony Woodford collection*

Above:
The opposite side of Bournemouth West, this time in sunny weather. The nearest vehicle is a Hillman Husky, in its typical grey and white paint scheme, and also visible is the back of an NCL yellow-liveried goods lorry. The main building is a collection of various styles which is indicative of expansion in previous decades. *Tony Woodford collection*

Left:
The rural charm of Oakley, west of Basingstoke, which nowadays stands as a private residence rather than a station. The line west from Basingstoke through to Andover and Salisbury is still open of course, although it must have been with more hope than certainty that such a stopping place could ever really have been expected to provide a financial return. The view is of the main approach which was on the up side. *Tony Woodford collection*

Above:
The magnificence of the former South Western Hotel at Southampton Terminus – the station of the same name is at the extreme left-hand corner of the hotel. For many years the hotel was a stopover for the wealthy arriving or departing from the ocean-going liners, but as with sea travel, its importance diminished over the years. Fortunately, the structure survives, and after a period in use as offices for the Cunard shipping line and also local BBC services, it has now been converted into desirable apartments. *Tony Woodford collection*

Right:
We now turn from the stations and structures to the detailed items therein, starting at Barnstaple Junction with a typical LSWR sign, although perhaps unusually placed under the canopy. There is a tall stretcher cabinet alongside – something rarely modelled. Unusually, the sign itself still has the full LSWR initials picked out in white, compared with the alterations made at other locations where only the 'S' and 'R' would be identified. *Tony Woodford collection*

Left:
Warning signs from various eras at what was No 10 crossing on the original Southampton & Dorchester Railway, located between Lymington Junction and Holmsley, photographed on 28 March 1964.
John Bailey

Below:
Over 100 miles east was Westerham in Kent which is seen from the terminus looking back towards Brasted and Dunton Green. This branch earned some fame for a time as an abortive attempt was made to both save and reopen it. In reality, its fate was probably sealed long before then as the route was required for the M25 and much has now disappeared under the concrete and tarmac of the orbital motorway. *Paul Bodkin*

INFRASTRUCTURE AND DETAIL

Right:
The running-in board and gas lamp at Totton, west of Southampton and viewed from the pedestrian footbridge. There was also a level crossing for road traffic, the bane of both railway and road, although foot passengers at least could avoid the queues. The start of modernisation on the far platform is evident, with the provision of the yellow litter bin. *Dave Waldron*

Below:
At first glance an identical lamp, but a closer look reveals the standard has the typical barley-twist shape. In the background, the existence of a solitary wagon in the down sidings is perhaps indicative of the decline of the railway at Wimborne. Nowadays there is hardly any trace that a station and extensive yard had ever existed. *Paul Bodkin*

PUBLIC NOTICE

WITHDRAWAL OF CERTAIN PASSENGER & FREIGHT TRAIN SERVICES

BROCKENHURST TO BOURNEMOUTH via RINGWOOD
SALISBURY TO BOURNEMOUTH via FORDINGBRIDGE

The British Railways Board propose, subject to prior completion of the necessary licensing procedure, to discontinue all railway passenger services between Brockenhurst and Bournemouth, via Ringwood, and between Salisbury and Bournemouth, via Fordingbridge, with effect from Monday, 4th May, 1964. The British Railways Board also propose from the same date to withdraw freight train services from some of the stations concerned, as indicated below.

Stations from which passenger and freight facilities will be completely withdrawn.	Stations from which passenger services will be completely withdrawn.
DOWNTON	HOLMSLEY
BREAMORE	RINGWOOD
FORDINGBRIDGE	ASHLEY HEATH HALT
DAGGONS ROAD	WEST MOORS
VERWOOD	WIMBORNE

The following is a copy of the consent received from the Ministry of Transport —

1. "I am directed by the Minister of Transport to refer to the report of the Transport Users Consultative Committee for the South Eastern Area upon objections and representations relating to the proposals to discontinue all railway passenger services between Brockenhurst and Bournemouth, via Ringwood, and between Salisbury and Bournemouth via Fordingbridge, and the discontinuance of all railway passenger services from the stations at Holmsley, Ringwood, Ashley Heath Halt, Downton, Breamore, Fordingbridge, Daggons Road, Verwood, West Moors, Wimborne, Broadstone and Creekmoor Halt. These proposed discontinuances are referred to in this letter as "the closures".

2. The Minister has considered the report of the Consultative Committee and all other relevant factors, including plans for development in the area. He accepts the view of the Committee that having regard to the bus services at present being provided no appreciable hardship to the

(ii) Whenever the Board become aware:

(a) of any proposal for an alteration of any of the bus services at present being provided which are set out in Part I of the Annex hereto (whether they are being provided by the persons named in Part I or by any other person) or of the additional bus services set out in Part II of the Annex by withdrawing or substantially reducing the frequency of any such service, or

(b) of any such alteration having been made,

the Board shall forthwith notify the Minister of any such proposal or alteration and give him all such information with respect thereto as he may reasonably require.

(iii) The Board shall take reasonable steps to keep themselves informed of

Above:

An unusual sign in that it depicts a boundary change rather than the more usual mileage. The location is Latchmere Junction with the SR route leading towards Longhedge. *Tony Goodyear*

Above:

A more conventional use of the same type of support post, which bearing in mind this is a book on the Southern, can only be one location, Padstow, the furthest west ventured by the SR. The enamel trespass notice in the background is perhaps a little unusual as most boards of this type were cast-iron. *Tony Woodford collection*

Left:

It is now an almost forgotten fact that the former LSWR had a major engineering works at Wimbledon in the early years of the 20th century. From here came many of the water tanks and equipment used throughout the system, all of which were also identified as such. This particular tank was at Basingstoke and disappeared, complete with its sign, at the same time as the abolition of steam traction. Similar signs existed on water tanks large and small on countless LSWR lines. *Tony Woodford collection*

Above:
The bare platforms of Allhallows-on-Sea, terminus of a line which opened as late as 1932. Unfortunately, anticipated development in the area never fully materialised and this little branch had a brief and uninspiring career, being closed less than 30 years later, in 1961. The canopy is typical of the SR building style which was utilised throughout the system for new works and rebuilding around that period. *Tony Woodford collection*

Left:
One of a pair of well-known signs which for many years, adorned the bridge over the expanse of railway just north of Southampton Terminus. Within the local area both signs were revered and admired, but have disappeared in recent years – one hopes with official sanction and safe retention?
Paul Bodkin

Right:
Another sign familiar to many was that at the south end of the island platforms at Eastleigh station, depicted on 8 June 1963. This was one of a pair which seemed to have the desired effect as even in the 1960s it was unusual to see staff walking across the myriad of lines in the area. They were removed commensurate with the cessation of steam working. *John Bailey*

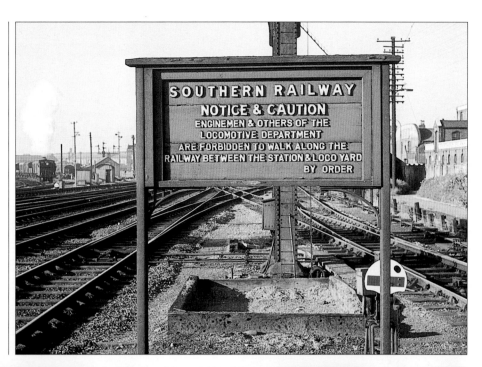

Below:
What is believed to have been a unique design of signalbox at Daggons Road with its curious curved roof covered in tarred canvas, seen on 8 July 1961. This location was on the line from West Moors to Alderbury Junction, near Salisbury, which closed in 1964. For many years this was classified as a ground frame and its origins may well have been with a local contractor. *John Bailey*

Above:
Former LSWR 24ft 4-wheeled luggage van No 6 at Tisbury on 29 August 1964. This vehicle stood in the down sidings at the station for many years without ever apparently moving. It is believed to have acted as a store and is a good example of how non-passenger carrying stock would often survive for decades after being superseded from their original intended use. *Tony Molyneaux*

Above:
Plymouth Friary looks very busy, but the lack of nameboards gives a clue to the fact that for some time traffic had been concentrated on the former GWR station at North Road, and the former LSWR station has become little more than a stabling point for coaching stock. *Tony Woodford collection*

Below:
An early casualty among the 'Battle of Britain' class engines, was No 34068 *Kenley* which was withdrawn at the end of 1963 and cut up at Eastleigh in March the following year. The train, seen at East Grinstead in 1957, could well be a Tunbridge Wells to Victoria service, some of which also ran via Hever. *Bob Winkworth collection*

Below:
A work stained 'C' class 0-6-0, No 31588 recorded at Paddock Wood, with what is believed to be a Hawkhurst line train. The red livery on the coaches was standard in the 1950s for branch line services although this was later replaced with standard SR green. The mass withdrawal of early stock consequent upon electrification meant that some vehicles never received a further repaint.
Bob Winkworth collection

Above:
Ashford Works-built 'C' class No 31258 works hard on a coal train from the Kent collieries. It is often forgotten now that places away from Wales, the Midlands and the North produced coal in volume, and that the Kent coalfield remained active until the general recession in the industry about 20 years ago. *Bob Winkworth collection*

Left:
Again at Paddock Wood, but this time it is an example of an 'H' class 0-4-4 tank, No 31517 which is reposing in the bay platform. This engine was built in 1909 and lasted in service until 1961. *Paul Bodkin*

Above:
The end of steam on the Eastern section nears as 'D1' class 4-4-0 No 31749 is seen on a set of green stock at Folkestone with a conductor rail in the foreground. For many years this engine was allocated to Stewarts Lane but in its final days was based at Bricklayers Arms from where it was withdrawn in November 1961 along with many a casualty of the electrification of the Kent Coast lines. *Bob Winkworth collection*

Below:
A delightful view of 'U' class 2-6-0 No 31615 at Dorking Town on a Reading–Tonbridge working in 1964. Steam-hauled services on this route sometimes used GWR locos in latter days, but usually only as far as Guildford. *Bob Winkworth collection*

Above:
Another Reading–Tonbridge line working, this time with 'E1' class 4-4-0 No 31506 seen near North Camp (Farnborough) in May 1957 with three-coach Maunsell set No 229, comprising two brake-thirds and a composite. *Bob Winkworth collection*

Below:
Two 'R1' class 0-6-0 tank engines hard at work on the steep, 1-in-36 gradient of the Folkestone Harbour branch in July 1958. Depending on the weight of the train it could be three engines pushing at the rear. In later years, former WR pannier tanks were utilised on this duty. *Bob Winkworth collection*

Right:
The final view in this sequence of former
South Eastern lines illustrations was recorded
at New Romney where 'H' class tank
No 31324 is seen at New Romney &
Littlestone-on-Sea. This short branch
diverged off another equally short branch to
Dungeness, and was accessed from the main
line at Appledore. *Bob Winkworth collection*

Below:
The rural charm of the branch line is typified
here with a 'T9' class 4-4-0 at the head of a
short freight train traversing the Meon Valley
route south of Alton. This line was an early
casualty with passenger services ceasing in
1955, but its limited patronage meant it was
perhaps surprising it had lasted that long.
Some freight continued to be handled
at both ends of the route until the mid-1960s
although as can be seen here, even that type
of traffic was limited. *S. C. Townroe*

Above:

A wet day on the north Cornwall coast, at the terminus station at Bude which, like Padstow, was another far-flung outpost of Southern influence. Two engines, 'N' class 2-6-0 No 31865 and BR Standard Class 4 2-6-4T No 80064 are present, the latter seemingly ready to depart for Halwill Junction. An oft-quoted rumour was that Waterloo wished for many years that they could hand over all their routes west of Exeter to Western Region control. However, when that did eventually occur the result was wholesale decimation with Bude being just one of many towns now devoid of rail connection. *Paul Bodkin*

Below:

Southern Railway concrete fittings dominate this view of 'M7' class 0-4-4T No 30667 ready to depart from Swanage for Wareham. On the left is the goods shed, the loco department and turntable being further north, beyond the bridge and on the right. Services on this line were eventually taken over by diesel-electric multiple units (DEMUs) but it was destined to close shortly afterwards. Fortunately, the station site and building survived and have now been resurrected as part of the very successful Swanage Railway. *Paul Bodkin*

Right:
'M7' No 30125 on the Lymington branch, believed *c*1960. This short line from Brockenhurst had the distinction of being the last steam-worked branch on BR and more recently has seen 'heritage' slam-door electric multiple-units operating a shuttle service between the two points. During steam days, and even for a while under more modern traction, there were through trains to and from Waterloo. These ceased some years ago and all passengers destined for Lymington are compelled to change trains at Brockenhurst. Had the plans of the 1940s come to fruition then there would have been a more direct route between Brockenhurst and Lymington, allegedly identified as a simple straight line drawn on a map by American engineers. 'We start Monday', was their comment, although that Monday never came and the original route, via lines opened in 1858 and 1884, still survives. *John Bailey*

Below:
We now look at the secondary services, commencing with the 6.2pm through service between Littlehampton and Totton recorded behind 'U' class 2-6-0 No 31620 at Netley on 20 July 1959. *John Bailey*

Left:
This is Portsmouth & Southsea High Level station on 18 April 1960 as 'U' class No 31794 heads the 11.37am Portsmouth Harbour–Cardiff. The coaching stock indicates this to be an inter-regional working, possibly from Liverpool. *John Bailey*

Below:
Rarely recorded in colour were the 17 members of the 'K' class 2-6-0s which were the main freight engines of the LBSCR. Here, No 32345 heads east at Burnetts Lane overbridge between Eastleigh and Botley while working an Eastleigh to Chichester freight on 13 October 1962. The stroke of a pen would see the complete class withdrawn *en bloc* just a short time later with no survivors; the type was deemed too heavy for the Bluebell Railway at the time. *John Bailey*

SECONDARY SERVICES AND ROUTES AND THE BRANCH LINES

Right:
A delightful group of warning signs advise motorists and pedestrians of what is perhaps the obvious hazard. The location is Trotts Lane on the Fawley branch with BR Standard Class 2 2-6-2T No 82012 having charge of the 6.43pm Fawley to Eastleigh passenger service on 7 May 1959. *John Bailey*

Below:
The staggered platforms at Lyndhurst Road station are the location here as BR Standard Class 5 No 73118 *King Leodegrance* heads west with a Bournemouth line service on an unreported date. As with so many wayside stations, Lyndhurst Road lost its local goods facilities in the early 1960s. Today, the station has been renamed Ashurst New Forest which is more appropriate for the adjacent village. *John Bailey*

Above:

BR Standard Class 5 No 73169 makes a powerful combination with rebuilt Pacific No 34077 *603 Squadron* as they pass Itchen Abbas with a diverted Waterloo to Bournemouth train on 1 May 1966. Double heading on the Southern was unusual, although certainly not unknown. One reason on this occasion could have been the severe gradients on the diversionary Mid-Hants route, but another may well have been the mechanical condition of the engines involved if it was similar to their external state. *John Bailey*

Left:

On the same date, 'West Country' class Pacific No 34002 *Salisbury* was captured at the top of the climb near Medstead with a diverted Waterloo–Bournemouth train although this time single-handed. Unfortunately, the angle of the view does not give any idea as to the length of the train being hauled, likewise the steepness of the grade – although this was 1 in 60 at this point, hence the nickname for the route, 'Over the Alps'. *John Bailey*

On the duty for which the class was intended, Maunsell 'S15' 4-6-0 No 30840 takes the West of England route at Worting Junction west of Basingstoke with a short freight. The use by the SR of route rather than train describing headcodes does not help to identify the type of service.
Tony Woodford collection

Below:
The unmistakable location of Barnstaple with 'West Country' Pacific No 34020 *Seaton* taking a three-coach train away from Ilfracombe. *Tony Woodford collection*

Above:
By the early 1960s, BR Standard engines had taken over many of the inter-regional services on the Southern, including the Portsmouth–Cardiff workings. An example is seen here with Class 4 2-6-0 No 76069 coming off the Portsmouth line at St Denys, heading south towards Southampton with a train bound for Salisbury and Cardiff on 3 June 1962. *John Bailey*

Below:
Meanwhile, back at Swanage, it is the bay platform that plays host to 'M7' No 30108 while it waits time for a return to Corfe Castle and Wareham. The fact this platform was being used indicates a second train was due to arrive – possibly a summer Saturday service, which would use the main platform on the left. The Wareham service will then depart as soon as the single line becomes free. *Paul Bodkin*

Above:
This appears to be an amalgam of two separate freight trains conjoined to save a locomotive and crew. This assumption is based on the fact that the front half of the train is purely petroleum tank wagons, while the rear portion is a mixture of other vehicles. The location is Allbrook, north of Eastleigh, and BR Standard Class 4 2-6-0 No 76060 is slowing ready to enter the yards at this point, on 10 June 1965. *Tony Molyneaux*

Below:
In charge of this freight at Millbrook is Southern-design 'U' class 2-6-0 No 31795 on what could be a pick-up goods on 20 July 1961. The station is in the background which possessed a single island platform serving the local lines seen in the centre. The fast lines were on either side and were not equipped with platform faces. *Tony Molyneaux*

Above:

The distinctive sight – and sound – of a train of banana vans leaving the old docks at Southampton with steam-heated vehicles behind 'U' class No 31809. This would have been destined for Nine Elms goods depot after which the product was despatched to the Covent Garden market – today located on the site of the former Nine Elms loco depot.
In the days before containerisation, boxes of bananas were craned off the ships and then manhandled into stacks in the railway wagons and again at the final destination.
Tony Molyneaux

Below:

Amidst the rolling countryside of North Devon, Ivatt 2-6-2T No 41290 is recorded approaching Bideford with a local service on 2 August 1961. The use of a maroon-liveried WR vehicle as the first coach is of interest.
Tony Molyneaux

Left:
'T9' class 4-4-0 No 30718 was photographed at Yeovil Junction on 14 August 1960 in charge of the RCTS 'Greyhound' special. *Tony Molyneaux*

Left:
Further west, 'N' class 2-6-0 No 31831 was captured near Mortehoe on 1 August 1962. Not far from here was the summit of the line to Ilfracombe after which the route dropped sharply to the coastal terminus. *Tony Molyneaux*

Left:
Filthy dirty but still nevertheless impressive from the low angle, 'King Arthur' class No 30782 *Sir Brian* waits in Platform 4 at Basingstoke with what is probably a Southampton Terminus to Waterloo stopping passenger service. This type of working was typical of those operated by these 4-6-0s in their last years, and they continued as such until ousted by the numerous BR Standard types. *Paul Bodkin*

SIGNAL BOXES

Below:
On the route west to Dorchester, a BR Standard Class 4, 76xxx series 2-6-0 passes the signalbox at Moreton, westbound, with a freight in the last days of steam. Hard by the signalbox but out of sight in the photograph was a level crossing which ensured the survival of the 'box until automatic half barriers were installed in 1972.
Bob Winkworth collection

Bottom:
What is now the renowned Southern Railway 'Greenhouse' type of signalbox design appeared throughout the system from the 1930s onwards. Several examples survive in use today, including Woking, Bognor Regis and as seen here, Templecombe. *Dave Waldron*

Above left:
An example of a small brick-built signalbox to South Western design and typified by this structure, at West Moors. Dating from the late 19th century, this was a typical LSWR design but without the centre brick or timber pillar, as seen in the example at Crow Crossing box later. *Paul Bodkin*

Above right:
Set at height so as to afford the signalman a good view through what was a curved layout, this is Christchurch LSWR signalbox dating from the 1885 and the opening of the Bournemouth direct line. Prior to then, the railway had served Christchurch and the eastern side of Bournemouth via a branch line from Ringwood. The importance of the Ringwood line diminished rapidly after this and it was closed early on, in 1935. *Dave Waldron*

Below:
Clapham Junction 'A' box recorded on 9 January 1960, unusually with an 'H' class 0-4-4 tank passing underneath on empty stock. Space constraints here dictated the only suitable location for the signalbox was above the tracks, and here it remained for many years until displaced by more modern equipment. In its later years its principal claim to fame was in 1965 when part of the structure collapsed, necessitating the temporary curtailment of all services in and out of Waterloo. Also in view is a 4-SUB EMU. *Paul Bodkin*

Above:

In a more rural setting, was the signalbox at Nursling on the route between Southampton and Romsey. Dating again from around 1885, the section controlled from here was regularly switched out of circuit in its later years, resulting in only one train at a time being able to run in either direction between Redbridge and Romsey. It was recorded by the photographer in this condition on 19 January 1963, hence the stop signal in the 'off' position and the snow on the roof; lack of roof insulation would have meant this would have quickly melted had there been a signalman in residence with a fire going. Unfortunately, the fact that Nursling was often unmanned did not go un-noticed with the local vandals and the box was eventually closed permanently, mainly due to wanton damage. *John Bailey*

Below:

A totally different type of structure, owing to its South Eastern Railway origins on the branch line to Hawkhurst. Goudhurst signalbox was responsible for the level crossing at the end of the station, and is seen painted in the then standard Southern Region green and cream livery. *Paul Bodkin*

Above:

A ground level centre-pillar LSWR box, located at Crow Crossing near Ringwood, photographed on 28 March 1964. This was on part of the original Southampton & Dorchester Railway which was beset with numerous level crossings, several with only a short distance between. Some, as here, were named while others were identified only by number. Out of sight in this view, but accompanying each structure, was accommodation for the crossing keeper and his family. *John Bailey*

Left:

This is Stockbridge on the erstwhile 'Sprat & Winkle' line, recorded on 27 June 1964. Despite being the most important intermediate station on the line, Stockbridge box was often switched out of circuit, the limited train service meaning there was little need for signalboxes every few miles. (On rural and cross-country lines signalboxes would usually be switched in for the day's shunting.)

Boxes that controlled level-crossings on this route were at Mottisfont, Clatford and Andover Town, and were in use continuously. At this stage in the line's life, the main lines can be seen still to be in use but it is clearly some time since the sidings have witnessed any traffic. *John Bailey*

Right:
The unusual brick design of Broadstone signalbox and the conference of the routes from Hamworthy, Branksome, Bailey Gate, and Wimborne. The train has come off the route from Branksome at Holes Bay Junction and appears to be heading towards Wimborne. The S&D line diverged off to the left, northwards towards Bailey Gate.
Tony Woodford collection

Below:
The BR successor to the LSWR centre-pillar type of signalbox is seen at Shalford, near Guildford in 1966. It had been policy on the Southern Region – and indeed elsewhere on BR – to place the lever frame facing towards the rear of the box whenever possible, and in so doing, affording the signalman an uninterrupted view of traffic. Replacement frames fitted in older boxes were often similarly sited. *Tony Goodyear*

Left:
Longhedge Junction signalbox is shown in its latter years with the locking room windows bricked up. This alteration was often a wartime precaution although even many years later – this view was taken in November 1977 – the difference in colour of the bricks could still be seen. The structure owes its origins to LBSCR design although a number of modifications have been made over the years. *Tony Goodyear*

Below:
An 'adopted' box on 29 July 1957, this is Upwey and Broadway near Weymouth which was formerly a Great Western route later taken over by the Southern Region. The impact of the green and cream signs of ownership are obvious and would have compared strikingly with the previous ones of 'light and dark stone'. *Paul Bodkin*

Right:
The interior of Stewarts Lane signalbox which has what appears to be a Westinghouse frame. The box also contains a mix of the old and the more modern, the numerous short levers operating colour light signals while a train describer can also be seen. The clock, however, is pure Southern Railway.
Tony Goodyear

Below:
New, 1960s technology: the panel at Sittingbourne recorded on 20 May 1962. This controlled the section from Sittingbourne to Sheerness-on-Sea and as can be seen, was fully track-circuited throughout. The black switches on the top of the panel operated the points individually, usually for maintenance, when required. *Tony Goodyear*

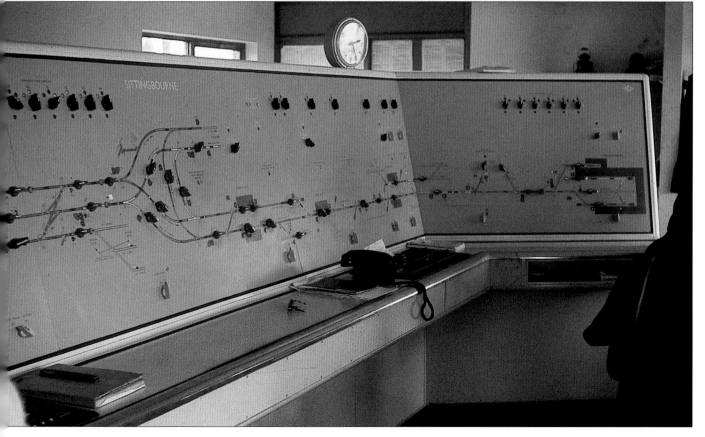

Below:
Characteristically LSWR, the up starting signal at Verwood complete with its painted sighting board on the brickwork 28 February 1964. Even so, this cannot have been an easy signal to spot, but with train crew having knowledge of the route, and train speeds limited, it is doubtful if the position of such signals was ever a serious hindrance to services. *John Bailey*

Above:
On the former LBSCR route between London Bridge and Sutton, this is the Tulse Hill up main starting signal with Knights Hill distant underneath. The signal is mounted on a complete Brighton and South London ac electrification overhead line gantry. The Herne Hill spur starting signal is mounted separately to the left. Knights Hill Tunnel can be seen in the background. *Tony Goodyear*

Below:
Former LSWR pneumatic signals at Brookwood in May 1964 with both the up main and up slow in the 'off' position. In the background approaching from the direction of Woking is 'S15' class 4-6-0 No 30835 with a down freight. The branch line to Bisley and the Necropolis line diverged from the main line at the other end of the station.
John Bailey

Right:
A more modern type of gantry at Worting Junction, west of Basingstoke where re-laying is taking place on the up fast line. The date is not recorded although it must be 1966 as conductor rail is in place on the right, although yet to be energised. On the extreme left is a group of railway cottages which still stand today. *Tony Woodford collection*

Below:
Southern design upper quadrant signals at Yeovil in BR days. The use of lattice for signal posts was commonplace on the SR while similar, although not identical posts could be seen on occasions on the Great Western. *Dave Waldron*

Below right:
An example of a tall LSWR post with co-acting lower arm seen at Totton outside Southampton. This was probably one of the last examples of its type to survive and certainly outlived the steam engine; the third rail is in place. The bracket for the lower arm was provided due to the curve of the track and platform canopy. Co-acting arms similar to this were once commonplace with most railway companies on fast lines, but had generally gone out of fashion by the 1950s, being replaced by banner repeaters located some distance in rear of the main signal. Similar banner repeaters, although either electrically operated or in the form of LEDs, are still in use today. *Dave Waldron*

Left:
Until the advent of privatisation the railway had been prepared to maintain a fleet of breakdown cranes to deal with emergencies and heavy engineering renewals. In more recent years, though, questions were asked as to the financial necessity of having expensive equipment standing idly by for much of the time and in consequence, there are few if any rail-borne cranes still in service. Depicted is No DS80, the former Guildford-based 36-ton steam crane, although on the occasion this view was recorded, in 1960, the machine was stationed at Eastleigh to provide cover for that depot's own crane which was temporarily out of service. *W. Bishop*

Below:
In addition to the cranes used by the motive power department, the civil engineers had their own cranes for lighter work which included track renewals. An example of this is seen taking place at Bevois Park sidings near Southampton where a complete track panel is being hoisted aloft while a DEMU passes in the background. Although clearly the BR Blue era, there is not a single high-visibility jacket to be seen. *Tony Woodford collection*

Right:
A sight not often seen was when the extension jib was attached to the Eastleigh crane specifically to allow it to reach a higher level. This was necessary on occasions such as when renewing the chimneys on the Eastleigh Works foundry, which were the exterior shells of former boiler barrels. Eastleigh fitters recall that it would take almost two days to modify the breakdown crane for this use and a similar amount of time to remove the extra jib afterwards. Despite this being a pre-planned operation, it meant the crane was effectively unavailable for breakdown use during this period. *W. Bishop*

Above:
A different type of crane is seen here, consisting of a travelling girder crane in the wheel-yard at Eastleigh Works. Aside from the line of wheelsets a number of vehicles in varying stages of store or repair are visible including VEP and SUB units. *Tony Woodford collection*

Below:
Adjacent to the site of the former Redbridge sleeper works on the outskirts of Southampton there was for many years an exterior stack of sleeper timbers, either ready for use or considered life-expired. Modernisation has reached out even as far as the humble sleeper, as for some time now concrete has been the favoured material for both plain track and more recently for turnouts, whenever track renewal is required. *Paul Bodkin*

Above:
Renowned as the finest brake vans ever to be built in Britain, this is an example of the 1936 Southern-design bogie type recorded half a century later, in departmental service. Affectionately known as 'Queen Marys', the original bogie vehicles of this type were rebuilds of former LBSCR overhead electric motor coaches with the conversions being so successful that a new build took place. Compared with the original conversions, the 1936 batch was not fitted with side windows. *Dave Waldron*

Left:
An expensive incident: a rake of Mk1 full-brake vehicles destroyed by fire between Eastleigh and Botley in 1962. The train had consisted of newspapers and parcels from Waterloo to Portsmouth and came to an abrupt halt in the countryside between the two stations in the early hours due to the communication cord being pulled when a fire was noted. Unfortunately, it proved impossible to uncouple the burning vehicles successfully with the result that the majority of the train was destroyed. If this was caused by a spark from the engine it was never confirmed. The inaccessibility of the incident can be gauged by the position of the fire engine in open farmland. Indeed, by the time the fire crew arrived there was little they could do, save mount a salvage operation and even then, little enough was worth salvaging. *S. C. Townroe*

LOCOMOTIVES

Right:
Nearing the end of its days at Eastleigh on 9 September 1961, but from the amount of coal on the tender, 'Lord Nelson' class 4-6-0 No 30858 *Lord Duncan* looks almost ready for its next duty. In reality, however, this would never come as it was recorded alongside the south side of the running shed, and despite having its name and number plates intact, had in fact already been withdrawn a few weeks earlier. *Tony Molyneaux*

Below:
In comparison, in May 1961, Eastleigh Works was still overhauling 'Terrier' 0-6-0Ts. No 32662 is seen ready for a return to its home shed of Fratton where it had a regular turn working the Hayling Island branch from Havant. The smart, lined-black livery suited these diminutive engines well. In the background can just be seen another 'Lord Nelson', this time No 30862 *Lord Collingwood* which was one of two members of the 'LN' class to survive the longest, until October 1962. *Les Elsey*

Above:
Two Maunsell designs at Basingstoke shed in the early 1960s, with No 30862 *Lord Collingwood* on the right, while nearest the camera is 'Schools' class No 30936 *Cranleigh*. It was unusual to see an 'LN' on Basingstoke shed although the 'Schools' were at this time working regularly on Basingstoke and Salisbury services having been displaced from the Kent Coast lines. The subsequent fate of No 30862 is mentioned in the previous caption, while the 'V' class 4-4-0 did not last much longer and was gone by December 1962, the duties once performed by these engines being taken over by BR Standard types. *Tony Woodford collection*

Below:
The rear of Eastleigh shed with BR Standard '9F' class No 92155 in temporary residence. The 2-10-0s were regular visitors to the area: they were seen at Bournemouth off the Somerset & Dorset line and also at Eastleigh yard having worked oil tank trains to and from the Midlands. They were prohibited from the Fawley branch however, hence engine changing was necessary at Eastleigh. What is not so widely known is that at least two members of the class were also sent for overhaul at Eastleigh Works in 1964. *John Bailey*

Above:
The sad sight inside Salisbury shed in the autumn of 1967. At first glance it appears as if it is simply a line-up of engines awaiting their next duty, but closer inspection reveals all have their rods removed and have been withdrawn. Aside from this though, their external condition at least appears reasonable. None from this final batch of engines would ever steam again as they were scrapped almost immediately upon reaching the South Wales dismantlers. *Bob Winkworth collection*

Below:
Ready for its last duties, 'Q' class 0-6-0 No 30548 with snow plough attached, was recorded at Eastleigh on 12 September 1964. Possibly this was a test fitting as it would certainly appear a little late in the year for a semi-permanent attachment. This was one of the class based at Eastleigh which found regular employment on local goods work in the area. A snowplough severely restricted its operational usefulness and took some time to both attach and remove. *John Bailey*

Above:
Brightness amidst a sea of grey: two variants of green livery, the restored 'T9' No 120 outside the rear of Eastleigh shed in company with 'USA' class 0-6-0 tank No DS238 *Wainwright*. The former LSWR 4-4-0 had been selected for official preservation and was in occasional use on special workings, while the 'USA' was allocated to departmental use. *Tony Woodford collection*

Left:
A Hampshire-based 'Terrier' on its home ground: No. 32650 at the terminus at Hayling Island, complete with a spark arrester. The truly diminutive size of these engines can be gauged even when they were standing alone – for example, the buffers are set above the centre line of the bufferbeam. The Hayling Island trains were the last regular passenger duties for the class in main line service, with some of these engines already over 80 years of age. *Tony Woodford collection*

Above:
A celebratory outing for enthusiasts at Newhaven on 12 April 1958. Tender-first and furthest from the camera, is the last surviving Brighton 'Atlantic', No 32424 *Beachy Head*, while nearer, are 'Terriers' Nos 32636 and 32640. The 'H2' class 4-4-2 had brought an RCTS special train from Victoria and had handed over to BR Standard Class 4 2-6-4T No 80154 (the last locomotive built at Brighton Works), for the short journey to Brighton. 'King Arthur' No 30796 *Sir Dodinas le Savage* then hauled the tour back from Brighton to Victoria. *Tony Molyneaux*

Below:
Steam was a rarity on the former South Eastern lines by the mid-1960s, although at first glance it certainly appears to be well represented at Ashford Works on 14 May 1964. In fact, these engines were works shunters, with two 'USA' class 0-6-0 tanks, Nos DS237 and DS238 in company with 'C' class 0-6-0 No 31271. *John Scott-Morgan*

Above:
Against the backdrop of the Horsham roundhouse on 21 August 1954, 'D3' class 0-4-4 tank No 32390 is in the process of being turned. Originally carrying the name *St Leonards*, this engine was the solitary member of the class then remaining in service and continued working local runs around the Brighton, Horsham, and Tunbridge areas until finally withdrawn in September 1955. None of the type was preserved.
Bob Winkworth collection

Below:
In smart plain black livery 'C' class 0-6-0 No 31686 is depicted alongside the ash-road at Hither Green depot. Members of this class were the last steam engines to work from the depot and aside from goods work from the nearby yard, were retained for special workings.
Bob Winkworth collection

Right:
En route from Eastleigh, possibly heading towards Guildford, 'USA' class No 30064 passes the shed at Basingstoke, some time in the early 1960s. The short wheelbase of this type meant that any attempt at anything other than slow running was, to say the least, uncomfortable for the crew while the bearings were prone to run hot. That said, they were ideal for shunting in Southampton Docks where sharp curves abounded. In later years, they were deemed as having the requisite power to act as shed pilots when required.
Tony Woodford collection

Below:
The mainstay of freight workings on the Brighton line were the 'K' class 2-6-0s, whose operational range slowly extended in consequence, first through the advent of the Southern Railway and then BR. All survived into BR days and carried lined-black livery well. No 32351 was photographed awaiting its next duty, during 1959.
Bob Winkworth collection

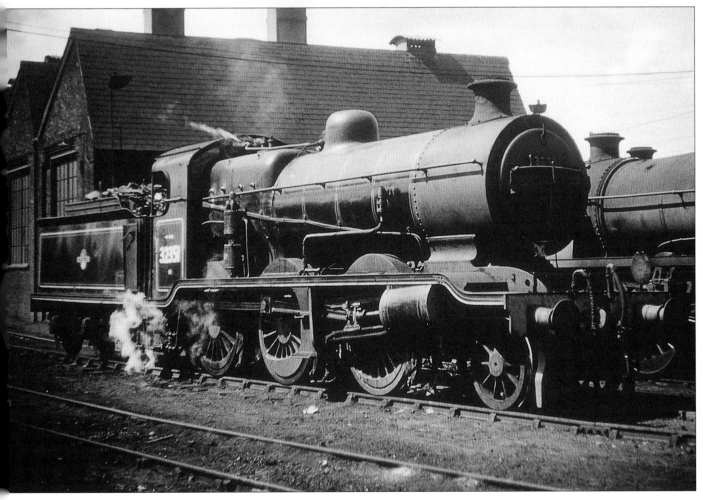

Above:
An impressive sight looking out towards the front of Eastleigh shed on 30 April 1967. Two 'West Country' class engines, Nos 34018 *Axminster* and 34024 *Tamar Valley* can be seen, the former having a chalked smokebox numberplate. Alongside to the right, is a 'Merchant Navy', easily recognisable from the shape of the nameplate. It was unusual to find an engine with a nameplate still attached at this late stage, most having been removed by the railway to prevent pilfering.
Collection Bob Winkworth

Below:
Clean and sparkling outside Eastleigh shed in May 1966, 'Battle of Britain' 4-6-2 No 34066 *Spitfire* is depicted in its final condition complete with AWS battery box and speedometer drive visible. Unfortunately, this was also the time when any defect not easily repairable would spell the end of an engine, and so despite its apparent excellent condition, the engine was withdrawn from traffic just four months later. No 34066 had been the standby engine at Waterloo for the funeral of Sir Winston Churchill in January 1965. *Bob Winkworth collection*

Above:
Still impressive even if covered in grime, Rebuilt 'Battle of Britain' No 34052, formerly carrying the name *Lord Dowding*, waits at Eastleigh in company with another equally grimy Pacific on 21 November 1966. Again, the AWS box and speedometer drive are evident, while it was just possible to see a small amount of green under the overall grime. *Bob Winkworth collection*

Below:
On the same date, No 34071 *601 Squadron* was seen at Eastleigh alongside the soon to be demolished coal stage at the depot. For the final few months the coaling of engines was accomplished here by a crane, the space of the former coaling stage required for an extension to the adjacent diesel depot. *Bob Winkworth collection*

Above:
The now-preserved Rebuilt 'Merchant Navy' No 35028 *Clan Line* at Weymouth depot on 29 April 1967. Weymouth had been built as a GWR shed but for its final years of operation was occupied in the servicing of former SR types. No 35028 is seen devoid of nameplates here, but these were restored for the final special workings in July 1967. *Bob Winkworth collection*

Below:
Former LSWR 'M7' No 30029 has been exiled from its home territory and is recorded receiving the attention of the cleaners at Tunbridge Wells West in March 1963. Exactly what the man with the bucket is doing on top of the firebox is not clear. The risk of falling from the side tanks is also obvious although despite the plethora of Health and Safety regulations affecting every aspect of our lives nowadays, accidents to cleaners and footplate crew on steam engines were few and far between. *Bob Winkworth collection*

Above:
'Battle of Britain' No 34061 *73 Squadron* at Eastleigh on 23 August 1964, exactly one week after having been withdrawn. As yet, the fitters have still to remove name and numberplates and the engine would still have one more trip to make, towed to Queenborough in Kent where it was dismantled in March 1965.
Bob Winkworth collection

Left:
Bournemouth shed yard, where there was a sign requesting drivers to keep their engines quiet as it was next to a residential area. How much notice the driver of Ivatt Class 2 2-6-2T No 41224 was taking of this as he shunted a rake of coal wagons in July 1967 is not certain. *Bob Winkworth collection*

Above:
The flats surrounding one side of Norwood Junction shed form the backdrop to this view of 'E6'class 0-6-2 tank No 32416, caught in the low sun of February 1958. Built at Brighton in November 1905, this was one of the original 12 engines of the class and remained in traffic until February 1962. *Bob Winkworth collection*

Left:
From one side of the system almost to the other now, and west to Yeovil shed where 4-6-0 No 30454 stands alongside an ensemble of Southern Region stock, but with a Great Western lower quadrant signal alongside. This locomotive was rebuilt from a Drummond 'G14' dating from 1914 and was subsequently given the name *Queen Guinevere*. Several of the type eked out their last regular workings on semi-fast duties on the West of England main line. *Bob Winkworth collection*

Above:
Amidst a sea of weeds, 'Merchant Navy' Class Pacific No 35008, formerly *Orient Line*, takes advantage of the over-girder turntable at Weymouth on 29 April 1967. The origins of Weymouth shed have already been mentioned, although if proof were needed, here is the painted evidence of chocolate and cream. *Bob Winkworth collection*

Right:
Surrounded by a mass of work-related items, No 34026 *Yes Tor* poses in a state of partial undress in Eastleigh Works. With the cladding removed, the clack valves and associated pipework are visible, along with the sandboxes. Ahead are the frames and cabside of 'Lord Nelson' No 30854 *Howard of Effingham* which, from its state of disassembly, is undergoing a full works overhaul. *Bob Winkworth collection*

Opposite top:
The other railway works in Hampshire was the permanent way foundry at Redbridge where rail chairs were cast. Some of the products made here are also visible while the heat and noise associated with such work can be well imagined from this scene with the furnace in the distance. *Paul Bodkin*

Right:
A final view of steam traction is this illustration of the nameplate and crest from 'Battle of Britain' class 4-6-2, No 34064 *Fighter Command*. From the sparkling appearance of the paintwork allied to the reflection, the engine was undoubtedly in ex-works condition, and was recorded as such by the photographer on 2 May 1964. *Tony Molyneaux*

Below:
The classic view of the rear of Eastleigh shed. Photographed on 4 March 1961, this was almost the last year when Maunsell types dominated the scene. After this time it was to be Bulleid and BR Standard types that were left in traffic. Clearly, the photographer was not the only visitor on this occasion, as the 'regulation' grey raincoat for the man on the right was typical enthusiast wear of the period. *John Bailey*

Left:
Think of the Southern Region in the late 1950s and 1960s BR era and the DEMU sets come to mind. With a bodyshell not dissimilar to contemporary electric multiple-units, the 33 original DEMUs were originally built as two-car sets but with the exception of Nos 1120-1122 were subsequently fitted with a centre trailer. Here, set No 1120 waits at New Romney, coupled to another of the type. *Tony Woodford collection*

Below:
The similarity with the electric units referred to is confirmed here as 2-HAP unit No 5618 leaves the confined end of Chatham station and enters the tunnel. Three-aspect colour light signalling is in place with track circuiting confirmed by the white diamond alongside. *Paul Bodkin*

Above:
It is early 1969 and the corporate blue livery has not yet reached this Class 25 Bo-Bo diesel-electric, which passes Peckham Rye with an inter-regional freight working. The short-wheelbase freight stock was itself on borrowed time and would totally vanish from the scene within a few years. *Tony Goodyear*

Below:
Coming off the Sutton line on the former LBSCR South London route, a 4-SUB EMU is seen passing the former electric car sheds at Peckham Rye in the early months of 1969. *Tony Goodyear*

Above:
Fresh from a repaint, a BRCW Type 3 D65xx series Bo-Bo diesel-electric (later Class 33), enters the down sidings at Basingstoke in August 1966. In the background are the two riding coaches from the Eastleigh breakdown train. The crane was present to lift the new signalling panel into the nearby power box which spelt the end of the semaphore signals in the distance. *Tony Woodford collection*

Left:
Deep in the West Country – unfortunately the photographer's records do not state where – Type 2 B-B diesel-hydraulic No D6312, one of a number of such engines which took over the former secondary routes of the LSWR/SR west of Exeter for their last years prior to closure. *Tony Woodford collection*

Right:
Mixed freight: 'Crompton' No D6526 running on the last leg of its journey from Didcot to Eastleigh south of Shawford in the summer of 1962. Most freights at this time contained a 'fitted head', meaning there was a reasonable amount of brake power available to the driver. The disadvantage, though, was that the poor old guard could still get knocked about due to the couplings snatching in the rear of the train. The acceleration capabilities of the diesels made this an all-too-common occurrence for freight guards of the period.
Tony Molyneaux

Below:
Coming off the Alton line at Winchester Junction and heading south is set No 1105. The DEMUs had taken over the duties of the former 'M7' and push-pull train sets on the Mid-Hants line although their reign was destined to be short-lived with the Alton line closing in 1973. *Dave Waldron*

Left:
Worting Junction, west of Basingstoke, as a 'Hampshire' DEMU running motor coach leads what is probably a Reading General to Southampton Terminus working. Nicknamed 'Thumpers' due to the ever-present drumming emanating from the engine, they developed a cult following in their last years, although this affinity was not often shared by those having no option but to use them for regular travel. The wires of the pole-route at this point are nothing short of superb, but being above ground were ever susceptible to both weather conditions and as time progressed, theft and vandalism. *Tony Woodford collection*

Below:
A variation in the Type 3 livery is seen on No D6563 running south of Eastleigh *en route* to Fawley on 11 March 1967. Other engines of the type were sporting either a small yellow warning panel or a yellow end which did not extend around the cab side windows. The third rail has been laid and energised with electric services having taken over certain workings. *Bob Winkworth collection*

Above:
Dieselisation at the Royal Pier, Southampton, as the flagman holds up a Ford Anglia Deluxe waiting to enter the Red Funnel compound. No D2989 (later Class 07) is running on the connecting line between the old and new docks, which for much of its distance, ran alongside the public road. This useful connection was later removed.
Collection Bob Winkworth

Below:
In green livery, a 'Hampshire' two-car DEMU crosses the new bridge over Redbridge causeway west of Southampton in July 1967. Just visible on the right of the tracks is the sleeper works referred to in previous views and also the small engine shed there. Redbridge was the location of the junction with the route to Romsey, while in the background, it is possible to see the cranes of what was to become the massive Southampton container port. *Bob Winkworth collection*

Left:
For a time in their earlier days, the 350hp diesel-electric shunting engines found a use on permanent-way trains, although more recently that type of work has been given over to larger engines. No D3666 is seen at Southampton Central on 21 February 1960 coupled to a track-laying machine.

While speed was not a necessity on these movements, the fact that the engines were restricted to a maximum of 25mph meant delays could well occur to other traffic arriving at and leaving the site of work.
John Bailey

Below:
One of the attractive Western region (WR) 'Cross-Country' diesel multiple units that for a time found employment on the Bristol–Portsmouth services, enters Platform 3 at Southampton Central on a very wet day in 1966. Much appreciated by passengers, these trains were considered extremely modern not only in their efficiency, but also in their appearance. They were, however, later replaced by diesel locomotive-hauled workings. *Dave Waldron*

Above:
Further replacement for steam in the West Country as a WR DMU pauses at Braunton station while parcels are transhipped. Such time-honoured work had been the province of the railway for decades, yet appears to have rarely been captured on film. Unfortunately, the view is not dated but from the overall blue livery of the three-car set was probably in the late 1960s. *Tony Woodford collection*

Below:
A rarely recorded phenomenon was diesel power on the S&D line. Here, Brush Type 2 (later Class 31) No 5824 has charge of five milk tank wagons, one of which is in St Ivel livery, at Bason Bridge, Somerset. Although milk traffic has been gone from the railway for many years, what may not be generally known is that during later BR days, a set of milk tankers was kept available on standby should an emergency occur resulting in road transport not being available. Indeed, the railways almost succeeded in recapturing this traffic again in the late 1980s, although not of course from locations such as Bason Bridge, which by that time had long ceased to have any rail connection. *Tony Woodford collection*

Left:
DEMU set No 1105 waits in the bay at Andover Junction ready to return down the route through to Romsey via Stockbridge. This picturesque little line, referred to as the 'Sprat and Winkle', was served by DEMUs during its final years and was at times well patronised, but unfortunately, Waterloo appeared determined to close it and eventually succeeded in 1964. In the background, a London-bound main line service enters the up platform. *Tony Woodford collection*

Below:
Diesel days at Worting Junction viewed from the vantage point of the overbridge, conveniently located at that point. The 'Warship' is working an Exeter service, while the BRCW Type 3 (Class 33) may either be waiting to follow or possibly routed south towards Winchester. Steam was still the mainstay of services at this time, the lack of conductor rails indicating this scene is in the period around early 1965. *Tony Woodford collection*

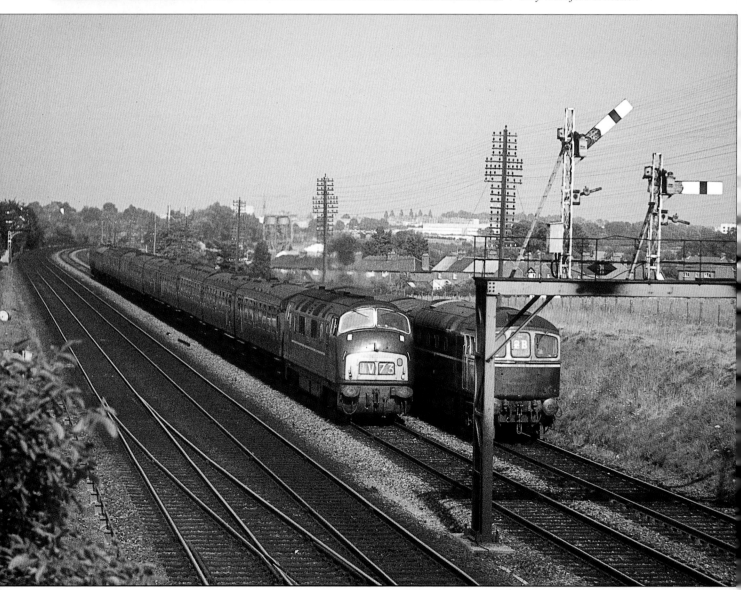

Right:
Photographed at the same point, 'Crompton' Type 3 No D6533 has charge of a down oil tank train returning from the Midlands towards Eastleigh and Fawley, on a sunny summer evening in 1965.
Tony Woodford collection

Below:
The film of rust on the rails indicates there was not a lot of activity at Northam Yard on this particular occasion – a bit different from nowadays, where the site has been cleared and is in use for servicing electric units. That was some time in the future as a three-car 'Hampshire' unit with the driving trailing leading, heads south past the signalbox of the same name. The junction here was for the lines to Southampton Terminus and Southampton Central, the latter taking a sharp curve around what was then a 20mph speed restriction. *Tony Woodford collection*

Above:
Replacement for steam at Basingstoke as two 4-TC sets, with No 401 leading, head south with a powered 'REP' set at the rear. The small yellow panel was short-lived and was soon replaced by a full yellow end. Likewise, the plain blue with aluminium fittings succumbed to the bland blue and grey of the 1970s. *Tony Woodford collection*

Below:
One of the big Class 74 electro-diesel locomotives passing Mount Pleasant near St Denys on a down fast. Never achieving quite what they had been intended to, these engines found limited use after electrification and by the late 1970s all had congregated at Eastleigh pending a decision as to their future. There would be no reprieve, and all of the type were scrapped. *Bob Winkworth collection*

Above:
Chertsey, 1 June 1970, and a minor collision occurred between a Class 74 electro-diesel No E6109 and a stationary 2-EPB unit No 5679. Fortunately the damage was negligible although the rail-borne crane was required to re-rail the end of the EMU. The crane is in the then-standard red livery for such equipment. *Tony Goodyear*

Right:
Permanent way work in progress as 4-REP No 3007 and a 4-TC set runs through Beaulieu Road station in 1968. The headcode '92' referred to the semi-fast service between Waterloo and Bournemouth and with the numerous stops and starts involved was a hard operation to run to time. *Dave Waldron*

Above:
A gathering of Class 33s at Eastleigh on one of the roads of the former steam shed. At least ten machines are visible, with what is probably a line of Class 47s behind. Such scenes were common for many years at Eastleigh, but later drew criticism from the occupants of the former railway cottages nearby due to the noise numerous engines would make ticking over as they slowly warmed up, particularly at night-time. *Bob Winkworth collection*

Below:
The unusual but by no means unique sight of two former 'Hastings' DEMU motor brake seconds being used as the depot shunter at St Leonard's West Marina. Such a requirement for motive power was necessary when EMUs were incapable of moving under their own power or needed to be shunted into non-electrified sidings. *Tony Goodyear*